23.95

LET'S EXPLORE THE STATES

Central Mississippi River Basin

Arkansas
Iowa
Missouri

Dorothy Kavanaugh

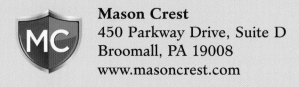

Mason Crest
450 Parkway Drive, Suite D
Broomall, PA 19008
www.masoncrest.com

©2016 by Mason Crest, an imprint of National Highlights, Inc.

Printed and bound in the United States of America.

CPSIA Compliance Information: Batch #LES2015.
For further information, contact Mason Crest at 1-866-MCP-Book.

First printing
1 3 5 7 9 8 6 4 2

Library of Congress Cataloging-in-Publication Data

Kavanaugh, Dorothy, 1969-
 Central Mississippi River Basin : Arkansas, Iowa, Missouri / Dorothy Kavanaugh.
    pages cm. — (Let's explore the states)
 Includes bibliographical references and index.
 ISBN 978-1-4222-3321-4 (hc)
 ISBN 978-1-4222-8606-7 (ebook)
 1. Arkansas—Juvenile literature. 2. Iowa—Juvenile literature. 3. Missouri—Juvenile literature.
 I. Title.
 F411.3.K38 2015
 976.7—dc23
                              2015012250

Let's Explore the States series ISBN: 978-1-4222-3319-1

Publisher's Note: Websites listed in this book were active at the time of publication. The publisher is not responsible for websites that have changed their address or discontinued operation since the date of publication. The publisher reviews and updates the websites each time the book is reprinted.

About the Author: Dorothy Kavanaugh is a writer and editor who lives near Philadelphia. She has written more than a dozen books for young readers.

Picture Credits: Architect of the Capitol: 11; Everett Historical: 53; Federal Emergency Management Agency photo: 30; Library of Congress: 15, 34 (top), 35, 42 (top), 59, 60; National Aeronautics and Space Administration: 42 (bottom); National Institutes of Health: 22 (bottom); used under license from Shutterstock, Inc.: 5, 6, 9, 10, 12, 16, 24, 26, 27, 32, 34 (bottom), 40, 47, 49 (top), 50, 58; American Spirit / Shutterstock.com: 1, 17, 29, 37, 39, 41; Creatista / Shutterstock.com: 43; Nagel Photography / Shutterstock.com: 19, 49 (bottom); R. Gino Santa Maria / Shutterstock.com: 57; Rena Schild / Shutterstock.com: 55; Stocklight / Shutterstock.com: 22 (top); Katherine Welles / Shutterstock.com: 20; The Woolaroc Museum: 13.

Table of Contents

KEY ICONS TO LOOK FOR:

Words to Understand: These words with their easy-to-understand definitions will increase the reader's understanding of the text, while building vocabulary skills.

Sidebars: This boxed material within the main text allows readers to build knowledge, gain insights, explore possibilities, and broaden their perspectives by weaving together additional information to provide realistic and holistic perspectives.

Research Projects: Readers are pointed toward areas of further inquiry connected to each chapter. Suggestions are provided for projects that encourage deeper research and analysis.

Text-Dependent Questions: These questions send the reader back to the text for more careful attention to the evidence presented there.

Series Glossary of Key Terms: This back-of-the book glossary contains terminology used throughout this series. Words found here increase the reader's ability to read and comprehend higher-level books and articles in this field.

LET'S EXPLORE THE STATES

Atlantic: North Carolina, Virginia, West Virginia

Central Mississippi River Basin: Arkansas, Iowa, Missouri

East South-Central States: Kentucky, Tennessee

Eastern Great Lakes: Indiana, Michigan, Ohio

Gulf States: Alabama, Louisiana, Mississippi

Lower Atlantic: Florida, Georgia, South Carolina

Lower Plains: Kansas, Nebraska

Mid-Atlantic: Delaware, District of Columbia, Maryland

Non-Continental: Alaska, Hawaii

Northern New England: Maine, New Hampshire, Vermont

Northeast: New Jersey, New York, Pennsylvania

Northwest: Idaho, Oregon, Washington

Rocky Mountain: Colorado, Utah, Wyoming

Southern New England: Connecticut, Massachusetts, Rhode Island

Southwest: New Mexico, Oklahoma, Texas

U.S. Territories and Possessions

Upper Plains: Montana, North Dakota, South Dakota

West: Arizona, California, Nevada

Western Great Lakes: Illinois, Minnesota, Wisconsin

Arkansas at a Glance

Area: 53,179 sq mi (137,732 sq km).
  29th largest state[1]
  Land: 52,036 sq mi (134,771 sq km)
  Water: 1,143 sq mi (2,961 sq km)
Highest elevation: Mount Magazine,
  2,753 feet (839 m)
Lowest elevation: Ouachita River at
  Louisiana border, 55 feet (17 m)

Statehood: June 15, 1836 (25th state)
Capital: Little Rock

Population: 2,966,369
  (32nd largest state)[2]

State nickname: the Natural State
State bird: Northern mockingbird
State flower: apple blossom

[1] *U.S. Geological Survey*
[2] *U.S. Census Bureau, 2014 estimate*

Arkansas

In 1995 the state of Arkansas adopted the nickname "the Natural State," to reflect its amazing natural resources: tall mountains, deep valleys, flowing rivers, dense woodlands, and fertile plains. Arkansas's scenic beauty and abundant wildlife help to make tourism one of the state's most important industries. But it is also a hub of industry and commerce, home to America's largest business as well as several other Fortune 500 companies.

Geography

Located in the southeastern United States, Arkansas covers an area of 53,179 square miles (137,733 square kilometers). It is the 29th largest state by area. Arkansas borders six other states. To the north is Missouri. The Mississippi River forms Arkansas's eastern border, separating it from Tennessee and Mississippi. Louisiana is located to the south. Oklahoma is located to the west, while Texas is to the southwest.

The geography of Arkansas varies widely. The state is covered by mountains, river valleys, forests, lakes, and bayous. Arkansas can be divided into three geographic regions: the northwest, the

Arkansas *delta*, and the southeast.

Northwest Arkansas includes the southern half of the Ozark Mountain range. Much of this area is covered with oak and hickory trees. The Ozark National Forest covers 1.2 million acres (490,000 hectares), and includes Arkansas's highest point, Mount Magazine, and two nearby peaks, Mount Nebo and Petit Jean Mountain. The Arkansas River runs through this region, as does the Buffalo National River, which since 1972 has been protected from development or the construction of hydroelectric dams by the National Park Service.

The Arkansas delta region is located east of the Ozarks and along the Mississippi River. Most of this region is low and flat, with fertile soil and swampy bayous. A broad *plateau* called Crowley's Ridge rises between 200 and 550 feet (61 and 170 m) above the delta lowlands. This formation is 150 miles (240 km) long and

 # Words to Understand in This Chapter

civil rights movement—an extended effort, conducted largely during the 1950s and 1960s, to secure for African Americans the rights of personal liberty guaranteed to all citizens.

delta—a triangular tract of sediment deposited at the mouth of a river.

nomadic—people who roam from place to place frequently, without establishing permanent settlements.

plateau—an area of relatively flat land that is raised sharply above adjacent land on at least one side.

poll tax—a sum of money that must be paid in order to be eligible to vote.

secede—to withdraw from a political union.

segregation—the practice of keeping white and black people apart in public.

A woman looks out across the Petit Jean River Valley from a large rock outcrop along the Ozark Mountain hiking trail in Mount Magazine State Park.

between half a mile (0.8 km) and twelve miles (19 km) wide. Most of the residents of the Arkansas delta region live in cities or towns on Crowley's Ridge, including the state's fifth-largest city, Jonesboro. The delta region is known for cotton production.

Southern Arkansas is sparsely populated, with much of this region covered by the pine and cypress trees of the Piney Woods. The woods are thick and dense.

In addition to the Arkansas River, which flows through the state, and the

Canoes on a bank of the Buffalo National River. The waterway is one of the few remaining rivers with no man-made dams in the 48 contiguous states. The river flows 135 miles (217 km), often cutting through massive bluffs on its way through the Ozark Mountains to the White River.

Mississippi, which forms the eastern border, Arkansas has four other major rivers. The Ouachita River and the Red River each flow southeast into Louisiana. The St. Francis River in northeastern Arkansas flows into the Mississippi River. The White River flows from northwest to southeast Arkansas.

Like other southern states, Arkansas has a warm climate. The average January high temperature in Little Rock is around 51° Fahrenheit (10° Celsius), while temperatures in July and August average around 93°F (34°C). It is cooler in the Ozark region, with average January temperatures around 46°F (8°C) and summer temperatures around 89 (32°C). Arkansas receives average rainfall of about 49.6 inches (126 cm). Some of the mountain areas receive about 5 inches (13 cm) of snow, but the delta and southern regions rarely see snow.

History

Approximately 14,000 years ago, the first humans crossed into North America from Asia via the Bering land bridge. These humans migrated south and spread throughout the continent, with some of them settling in the region that today is Arkansas. Descendants of these early inhabitants became various Native American tribes.

Most of the Native Americans were **nomadic**. They traveled through large areas during the year and hunted or fished for their food. However, by around the year 650 CE, some tribes had begun to settle into permanent villages and develop more complex civilizations. The built large mounds and earthworks as ceremonial and religious centers. Their culture and practices are known as Mississippian culture, and flourished from around 800 to 1600 CE. The Toltec Mounds site on the Arkansas river in central Arkansas includes the remains of the largest Mississippian site in the region.

Among the first Europeans to explore the area that today is Arkansas were members of a small army led by Hernando de Soto. After crossing the Mississippi River, the Spaniards trekked west through the area in 1541. In May 1542, while passing back through the region, de Soto died in Arkansas. His men buried him secretly in the Mississippi River

Spanish conquistador and explorer Hernando De Soto (1500–1542), riding a white horse and dressed in Renaissance finery, arrives at the Mississippi River on May 8, 1541. De Soto was the first European documented to have seen the river.

so that hostile Native Americans would not know that the feared Spanish leader was dead.

The next Europeans to explore the region were French. More than a century after De Soto, in 1682, the French explorer René-Robert Cavelier, Sieur de La Salle, led an expedition down the Mississippi River from present-day Illinois all the way to the Gulf of Mexico. La Salle claimed for France the Mississippi River and its entire drainage basin. That massive territory included a million square miles in the center of North America, including Arkansas, which La Salle named Louisiana.

La Salle's friend Henri de Tonti established the first European settlement in the region at Arkansas Post in 1688. It was located near the spot where the Arkansas and Mississippi Rivers converged. The trading post was a place where fur trappers and mountain men could trade with Native Americans.

The main tribes living in this region during the 18th and early 19th centuries were the Caddo, Osage, and Quapaw peoples. The Caddo lived in

Restored buildings at Arkansas Post, the first European settlement in the region. French and Spanish fur traders used the post to trade with Native Americans, particularly the Quapaw people. In 1819 Arkansas Post was designated the first capital of the Arkansas Territory, but it was replaced as capital by Little Rock two years later. Today, Arkansas Post is a national park.

villages along the Red River in the southeast. The Osage hunted in northern Arkansas, although most Osage villages were in what today is Missouri. The Quapaw were very friendly to the French. They lived in villages were near the mouth of the Arkansas River. The name *Arkansas* comes from *Akansea*, a French phonetic spelling of a Native American word for the Quapaw tribe.

In 1803, France sold its rights to the Louisiana Territory to the fledgling United States, which had been created when thirteen British colonies on the Atlantic coast of North America declared their independence from Great Britain. This purchase more than doubled the size of the United States. U.S. President Thomas Jefferson sent the Lewis and Clark expedition to explore the northern area of the new territory. Jefferson sent a less-well-known expedition, led by William Dunbar and George Hunter, to find the southern boundary of Louisiana. The Dunbar-Hunter Expedition explored the Red, Black, and Ouachita rivers and discovered the hot springs in central Arkansas.

During the first decade after the Louisiana Purchase, few white settlers came to Arkansas. In fact the largest immigrant group was the Cherokee Native American tribe, which was forced to leave its traditional lands in southeastern states like South Carolina, Georgia, and Tennessee due to the expansion of American settlements there. Large numbers of Cherokee came to Arkansas after the end of the War of 1812, and again in 1817. These Native Americans, and other tribes living in Arkansas would

During the 1810s, the U.S. government implemented policies that removed Cherokee Indians from their homes and and forced them to move to new lands in the west, including Arkansas and Oklahoma.

eventually be forced by the U.S. government to move to new lands farther west in Oklahoma.

Over time, the lands of the Louisiana Purchase were broken into different entities, called territories. Once a territory was formed, its residents could apply for statehood when certain conditions were met. The Arkansas Territory was formed in 1819. It included all of the present-day state, plus part of the land that would eventually become Oklahoma.

Like other southern lands, slavery was permitted in Arkansas. Slave labor was used on large cotton plantations in the southeastern part of the territory. In 1820, the Arkansas Territory had a population of about 14,000. By the mid-1830s, the territory's population had reached 60,000, making it eligible for statehood. The territory's leaders drafted a state constitution, and petitioned the U.S. Congress for admission to the United States. The state's present-day boundaries were set, with the western portion becoming part of what was then called Indian Territory (now Oklahoma). On June 14, 1836, Arkansas was admitted as the 25th state.

Although Arkansas was a slave state, its residents were somewhat divided on the issue of slavery. Many residents did not have slaves, as the crops that could be grown in the northeastern part of Arkansas did not require cheap labor. After the election of Abraham Lincoln in November 1860, seven southern states voted to *secede* from the Union and form their own country, the Confederate States of America. Arkansas residents, however, voted to remain part of the United States. However, when Lincoln refused to allow the southern states to secede, and asked Arkansas to send troops to Fort Sumter, South Carolina, to quell the rebellion there, state leaders refused. In May 1861, at a second convention, Arkansas leaders voted to join the Confederacy.

During the war Arkansas was strategically important because it could control river traffic on the Mississippi River, a vital lifeline for U.S. trade and commerce. Several

The Battle of Pea Ridge, fought in Arkansas, was an important Union victory. It halted a Confederate attempt to invade Missouri, and ensure that the state would remain under federal control.

important battles were fought in Arkansas, including the Battle of Pea Ridge in March 1862. Union forces eventually gained control of the major cities Helena and Little Rock. During the war, guerrilla fighting between Confederate sympathizers and Union supporters caused major damage throughout the state.

After the Civil War ended, the rebellious southern states had to go through a process known as Reconstruction before they could be fully restored to the Union. During the Reconstruction period, the U.S. Congress tried to reorganize the

Southern states and make sure newly freed blacks enjoyed full citizenship rights. Arkansas was readmitted in 1868 with a new constitution that allowed African Americans to vote and prohibited former Confederate leaders from holding office. Arkansas also established a statewide system of public education, open to children of all races.

However, political developments in Arkansas—especially in the matter of race relations—soon took a similar course to what occurred in many other Southern states. In the 1870s African Americans, as well as poor whites, were prevented from voting by the adoption of a ***poll tax***. Laws were passed that required blacks and whites to be ***segregated***, or kept apart, in public places. "Separate but equal" accommodations were supposed to be made for black and white people. But invariably the facilities provided for African Americans—the schools their children attended, the restaurant areas where they could eat, the restrooms they could use, and much more—were not equal. They were inferior to the facilities whites enjoyed. This system of legal segregation was known as Jim Crow, and it

This statue of the Little Rock Nine—the African-American students who integrated Central High School in 1957—is located on the Arkansas state capitol grounds.

Former U.S. presidents Bill Clinton, George W. Bush, Jimmy Carter, and George H.W. Bush approach the stage during the ceremony to open the William J. Clinton Presidential Library in Little Rock, November 2004.

helped ensure that African Americans would be second-class citizens. Jim Crow segregation would last until the *civil rights movement* of the 1950s and 1960s.

One landmark civil rights decision was the U.S. Supreme Court's ruling in the 1954 case *Brown v. Board of Education of Topeka, Kansas*, which declared that segregation in public schools was unconstitutional. Three years later, Arkansas attracted national attention when the federal government had to intervene to allow nine African-American students to attend Central High School in Little Rock.

When Arkansas Governor Orval Faubus refused to comply with the federal ruling, U.S. President Dwight D. Eisenhower sent military troops to escort and protect the African-American students.

In 1978, a young Arkansas native named William Jefferson "Bill" Clinton was elected the state's governor. Clinton's first two-year term was not a success, and he was voted out of office in 1980. However, Clinton would run for re-election and win in 1982, and serve nearly twelve years as governor. In 1992, Clinton became the first Arkansan to be elected president of the United States, defeating incumbent George H.W. Bush and third-party candidate Ross Perot. During his administration Clinton oversaw a period of great economic growth and was re-elected in 1996. Since leaving office in January 2001, he has generally been rated by historians as an effective and popular president.

Government

The current constitution of Arkansas was adopted in 1874. It replaced a state constitution written six years earlier, in 1868, when the state was readmitted to the Union after the Civil War. The state's government is patterned after the federal government, as it is divided into executive, legislative, and judicial branches.

The Governor of Arkansas is the head of the executive branch. He is responsible for making sure that the state's laws are enforced, and must approve or veto all new bills passed by the state legislature. The governor also appoints people to lead certain state departments. Governors are elected to four-year terms, and can serve two terms in office.

Unlike most states, in Arkansas the lieutenant governor is elected separately from the governor, and so can be from a different political party. The lieutenant governor helps to run the executive branch, and can vote to break ties in the state senate. If the governor resigns or dies while in office, the lieutenant governor assumes that position. Several other executive officers are elected by voters in Arkansas, including the secretary of state, treasurer, attorney general, auditor, and commissioner of state lands.

The Arkansas General Assembly is bicameral, consisting of two houses. The Senate contains 35 members, who can serve a maximum of two four-year terms. The House of Representatives has 100 members, who can serve three two-year terms. All representatives and half of the senators are up for election every two years. Both houses hold their legislative sessions in the Arkansas State Capitol building.

The judicial branch includes several court systems. Civil and criminal

Interior view of the House of Representatives chamber in the Arkansas State Capitol building in Little Rock.

cases are heard in the state's district courts, or in city courts associated with each district. Decisions in those cases can be appealed to one of the state's five circuit courts, and from there to the Arkansas Court of Appeals. The highest court in the state is the Arkansas Supreme Court, which consists of seven justices who are elected to eight-year terms.

Arkansas voters are represented in the federal government by two U.S. Senators and four members of the U.S. House of Representatives. The state casts six votes in the electoral college during presidential elections.

The Economy

Arkansas is home to several companies that are among the 500 largest U.S. businesses. The biggest of these is Walmart, based in Bentonville. This superstore chain, founded by entrepreneur Sam Walton, is the largest American company, with annual revenue of more than $470 billion.

Tyson Foods, with annual revenue of around $33 billion, is the largest American meatpacking company. It is based in Arkansas and operates many plants in the state, as well as in Iowa and other Midwestern states.

Entrance to the Walmart Home Office in Bentonville, the world headquarters of the retail giant. Founded by Sam Walton in 1962, the company today is the world's largest by revenue, and operates more than 11,000 stores in 27 different countries.

Murphy Oil Corporation is headquartered in El Dorado. It produces oil and natural gas in the United States, Canada, and many other countries around the world.

Some other major companies in Arkansas include Dillard's, a department store chain based in Little Rock that operates nearly 300 stores in 28 states; Windstream Communications, also headquartered in Little Rock, which provides phone, Internet, and television services to customers in the Southwest and has annual revenue of about $6 billion; and trucking firm J.B. Hunt, which employs more than 19,000 people and transports good all over the country.

Arkansas is also a leading state when it comes to aquafarming, or raising fish or seafood to be used as food. The primary aquaculture product is channel catfish. Arkansas was one of the first states to develop commercial catfish farms, and today these fish are raised throughout the state.

The People

In 1836, when Arkansas was admitted to the United States, the state had a population of about 60,000. By 2015, the population of Arkansas had grown to nearly 3 million, which ranked it 32nd among the 50 states.

According to the U.S. Census Bureau, about 80 percent of Arkansas residents are white. Blacks or African Americans make up 15.6 percent of the population, which is a little higher than the national average of (13.2 percent). African Americans mostly live in the southern and eastern parts of the state. There are small populations of Asians and Native Americans.

Arkansas is generally not a destination for immigrants. Residents who identify themselves as Hispanic or Latino (and can therefore be either racially white or black) compose about 7 percent of the population, well below the national average of 17 percent. Only about 4.5 percent of the state's population was born in another country, and just 7 percent speak a language other than English at home.

People in Arkansas graduate from high school at a slightly lower rate than the rest of the country (83.7 percent vs. the national average of 86 per-

cent), and are less likely to earn a college degree (20 percent vs. a national average of 28.8 percent). Perhaps due to this educational disparity, the median household income of about $41,000 is significantly below the national average ($53,000), and more than 19 percent of Arkansas residents have incomes below the federal poverty level.

Like most Southern states, Arkansas is part of the Bible Belt, a region in which the Protestant Christianity plays an important role in society and politics. About 78 percent of Arkansas residents describe themselves as Protestant Christian, with the Baptist and Methodist churches being the largest denominations. About 7 percent are Roman Catholic, while roughly 14 percent describe themselves as non-religious.

Major Cities

Arkansas's largest city is the state capitol, *Little Rock*, with a population of nearly 200,000. The city was founded in 1821 and has a long, rich history. Today, Little Rock is a major eco-

Some Famous Arkansans

William Jefferson "Bill" Clinton (b. 1946) is the only U.S. president from Arkansas, serving in that office from 1993 to 2001. Clinton had previously served as governor of Arkansas from 1979 to 1981 and from 1983 to 1992. Since leaving the presidency, Clinton has been involved in public speaking and humanitarian work.

Bill Clinton

Confederate general Patrick Cleburne (1828–1864) was an Irish immigrant who settled in Helena before the Civil War. Cleburne was nicknamed "the Stonewall of the West" for his military successes against much larger forces, and he was considered one of the best battlefield tacticians in the western theatre of the war. However, he angered Confederate leaders with a controversial proposal in 1864 that the South should free any slaves who were willing to fight against Union forces.

Musical icon Johnny Cash (1932–2003) was born in Kingsland and grew up on a cotton farm in Dyess. The singer-songwriter was one of America's most influential musicians, known for hits like "Folsom Prison Blues," "Ring of Fire," "One Piece at a Time," and "A Boy Named Sue." Several other major country music stars lived for part of their lives in Arkansas, including Conway Twitty (1933–1993), who recorded 40 number one singles, and Glen Campbell (b. 1936 near Delight), whose hits in the 1960s and 1970s included "Rhinestone Cowboy" and "Gentle on My Mind."

Dr. Joycelyn Elders (b. 1933), born in Schaal, became the first African American to serve as Surgeon General of the United States in 1993. Today she is a professor of pediatrics at the University of Arkansas.

The large family of Jim Bob (b. 1965) and Michelle (b. 1967) Duggar has gained national recognition due to their appearance on several reality television programs, including *19 Kids and Counting*. The family lives in Tontitown.

Joycelyn Elders

nomic and cultural center for the entire state, as well as being the home of most state government offices.

Little Rock's scenic location on the Arkansas River offers residents plenty of outdoor activities, including hiking, hunting, cycling, boating, and fishing. Little Rock is also home to many museums and fine art galleries, a symphony orchestra, and a performing arts center. The William J. Clinton Presidential Center and Park has the largest archive of any presidential library, and attracts speakers from all over the world. In 2013, Little Rock was ranked first among midsized cities in a list of "Best Places to Live" published by the business magazine *Kiplinger*.

Founded in 1817 as a military post, *Fort Smith* is Arkansas's second-largest city with a population of about 86,500. During the late nineteenth century, the city was home to U.S. District Judge Isaac Parker, who was known as the "Hanging Judge" for his tough frontier justice. The city is home to many manufacturing facilities. The Fort Smith Convention Center is one of the largest facilities in the state, and hosts many conferences and events.

Fayetteville, the state's third-largest city, has a population of about 77,000. The University of Arkansas, which enrolls about 26,000 students, has its main campus in Fayetteville, and there are numerous industries nearby. The small city is rated as being a very nice place to live, with extensive bike and pedestrian trails.

Located in the Ozark Mountains of northwestern Arkansas, *Springdale* (population 70,000) is an important industrial city. It is home to the world headquarters of Tyson Foods, the world's largest meat-producing company. Due to this connection, Springfield is sometimes called the "Poultry Capital of the World." The aerospace company Pratt & Whitney has a factory in Springfield as well.

Arkansas State University is located in *Jonesboro* (population 68,000), and this has helped to make the city a regional center for education and trade. Jonesboro is also noted as the home town of American novelist John Grisham.

One of the natural thermal springs that gives Hot Springs its name. Native Americans believed the waters had healing powers.

Other notable communities in Arkansas include **Conway** (population 60,000), where the University of Central Arkansas is located, and **Pine Bluff** (population 50,000), in southeastern Arkansas. **Bentonville** (population 35,500), located not far from Fayetteville, was the location of Sam Walton's first store. Today, the city is home to Walmart's national headquarters. **Hot Springs** (population 35,000), named for nearby thermal springs, was the boyhood home of former U.S. president Bill Clinton.

Further Reading

Levy, Janet. *Arkansas: Past and Present*. New York: Rosen, 2010.

Marsh, Carole. *I'm Reading About Arkansas*. Peachtree, Ga.: Gallopade International, 2014.

Prentzas, G.S. *Arkansas*. New York: Children's Press, 2014.

Internet Resources

http://arkansashistoricalassociation.org/

> The Arkansas Historical Association publishes the quarterly journal *Arkansas Historical Quarterly*, and provides access to the state's historical resources.

http://www.state.ar.us

> This is the official website for the State of Arkansas, and provides information about state and local government services.

http://www.arkansas.com

> The official tourism website of Arkansas provides information about places to visit and things to do in the state.

http://www.americaslibrary.gov/es/ar/es_ar_subj.html

> A page of interesting information about Arkansas, provided by the Library of Congress.

 # Text-Dependent Questions

> 1. What is the name of the broad plateau that is found in the Arkansas delta region?
> 2. When was Arkansas re-admitted to the Union during the Reconstruction period?
> 3. What are three of the six Fortune 500 companies that are headquartered in Arkansas?

 # Research Project

Using your school library or the Internet, read about the desegregation of Little Rock's Central High School in 1957. Write a few paragraphs explaining what happened. Describe how and why those nine African-American students were chosen to integrate the school, and discuss the the role of both the state and federal governments in this affair. Present your report to the class.

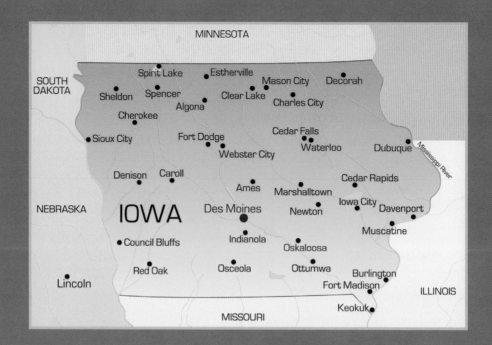

Iowa at a Glance

Area: 56,272 sq mi (145,743 sq km)[1]
(26th largest state)
Land: 55,857 sq mi (144,669 sq km)
Water: 416 sq mi (1,077 sq km)
Highest elevation: Hawkeye Point,
1,671 feet (509 m)
Lowest elevation: confluence of
Mississippi and Des Moines Rivers,
480 feet (146 m)

Statehood: December 28, 1846
(29th state)
Capital: Des Moines

Pop.: 3,107,126 (30th largest state)[2]

State nickname: the Hawkeye State
State bird: American goldfinch
State flower: Rosa arkansana

[1] *U.S. Geological Survey*
[2] *U.S. Census Bureau, 2014 estimate*

Iowa

Iowa is a predominantly agricultural state, with most people living on farms or in small towns and relatively few large cities. It is also a place where most people live stable, comfortable lives, where family relationships are strong, and where the quality of life is high. Because of its geographic location and strong traditions, many people consider Iowa to be "middle America" or the "heartland."

Geography

Iowa is the only U.S. state in which the eastern and western borders are formed entirely by rivers: the Mississippi River to the east, and the Missouri and Big Sioux rivers to the west. The state of Minnesota lies to the north; Wisconsin and Illinois are to the east; Missouri is to the south, and Nebraska and South Dakota are located to the west. It is the 26th-largest state by area, covering 56,272 square miles (145,743 sq km).

Most of Iowa is covered with rolling hills and rich soil that is ideal for farming, particularly in the southern half of the state. In the western part of the state are ancient soil formations known as the Loess Hills. They rise from 200 to 350 feet (61 to 110 m) above the plains of Iowa, forming a narrow band that roughly follows the path of the Missouri River. The Loess Hills run for about 200 miles (320 km), all the way to Mound City in northern Missouri. In many areas, the hills are covered with forests and prairie grass.

A small area in northeastern Iowa looks much different from the rest of the state, because it has large hills and steep river valleys. This area is wooded and attracts large flocks of migratory birds.

The state's highest point, Hawkeye Point, is located in northwestern Iowa not far from the Minnesota border. It rises 1,671 feet (509 m) above sea level. However, it is not a mountain that towers over the rest of the landscape. Instead, it rises gradually about 20 feet (6 m) above the surrounding farmland.

To the south of Hawkeye Point is a large marshy area known as Barringer Slough. This large area of wetlands covers 2.4 square miles (6.2 sq km). Many small animals and waterfowl live

Words to Understand in This Chapter

caucus—a meeting of members of a political party for the purpose of choosing candidates for an election.

cede—to formally yield or give up territory or power to someone else.

prototype—an early or preliminary form of something, such as a machine, from which later machines are developed or copied.

slough—a swampy area of soft, muddy ground and wetlands.

subsidy—a sum of money granted by the government to help an industry or business so that the price of a commodity can remain low or competitive.

Rolling farm fields in northeastern Iowa. The state is known for its agricultural production.

The Hogback Covered Bridge, built in 1884, is one of six remaining historic covered bridges in Madison County.

Iowa is sometimes subjected to flooding. These homes and businesses were flooded when the Skunk River rose due to heavy rains near Colfax in August 2010.

in the *slough*.

Most of Iowa's land is used for farming. Crops are grown on 60 percent of the state's land. Grasslands cover about 30 percent of the state; they are used for raising livestock, although there are some areas of native prairie grasses and wetlands as well. About 7 percent of Iowa is covered with forests.

Iowa has a temperate climate. The average January high temperature in Des Moines is around 31°F (–1°C), while temperatures in July average around 86°F (30°C). Iowa receives average rainfall of about 66 inches (91 cm).

Iowa is regularly affected by tornadoes, which occur practically every year. One of the worst recent storms occurred in April 2011, when dozens of tornadoes hit the state, causing more than $75 billion in damage.

Due to the state's proximity to major rivers, flooding is another natural disaster that regularly plagues Iowa. In the spring and summer of 1993, the Mississippi River flooded a huge area of the Midwest, including Iowa, destroying farms and crops. In

June 2008, the Mississippi flooded again, with an even higher crest than in 1993. Cedar Rapids and Iowa City received significant damage due to being inundated.

History

Many different Native American tribes lived in Iowa before the arrival of European-American settlers in the 19th century. In fact, the state's name comes from the Iowa (or Ioway) people. This Sioux tribe lived on the plains before the arrival of European settlers.

The largest tribes in this region the Sauk and Mesquaki, who inhabited a large area that covered parts of present-day Illinois and Iowa, along the Rock and Mississippi Rivers. These Amerindians were semi-nomadic. They lived in established villages during the winter months, but traveled through their territory during the spring and summer months hunting, fishing, and gathering supplies.

The first whites to reach the Iowa region were the French explorers Louis Joliet and Father Jacques Marquette, who traveled the northern portion of the Mississippi River in 1673. They stopped near the point where the Iowa River flowed into the Mississippi. In his journal, Marquette wrote that the land in this region was lush, green, and fertile.

By the end of the 17th century, the entire region had been claimed by France. However, the few whites who visited Iowa during this time were fur trappers or mountain men looking to trade with the Native Americans.

In 1803, France sold an enormous expanse of western territory to the United States. Iowa was part of this region, known as the Louisiana Territory.

As American settlers moved west, there was greater interaction with the Native Americans. This sometimes led to warfare, especially when the U.S. government forced Native Americans off their land. In 1832, the Sauk chief Black Hawk, angry about the loss of Sauk territory in Illinois, went to war against American troops. Ultimately, the U.S. military prevailed, and the Sauk were forced to permanently *cede* some of their territory in Iowa in what became known as the Black Hawk Purchase. It became part of the United States, as part of what was known as the Michigan Territory.

The first whites in Iowa settled in the Black Hawk Purchase area in 1833. These pioneers found that the terrain was much different from the forest-covered land to the east. Much of Iowa was covered in prairie grasses, rather than trees, so there was little convenient wood for building homes or to use as fuel. The settlers soon learned to build sod homes from blocks of earth. They used coal and prairie grasses to fuel cooking fires.

Despite these hardships, pioneers soon learned that there were great benefits to settling in the region, as the soil in Iowa was extremely rich and fertile.

By 1838, there were more than 22,000 American settlers in the Iowa region. This was enough for the U.S. government to establish it as a separate territory. The Iowa Territory included parts of present-day Minnesota, North Dakota, and South Dakota. The town of Burlington was established as the territorial capital, although in 1840 the capital would be moved to Iowa City.

The sun rises over the Des Moines River as it flows through the state's capital and largest city.

Settlement continued rapidly. By 1845, the population of the Iowa Territory had increased to over 75,000. Iowans applied for U.S. statehood. The state's present-day borders were established, with some of the western lands becoming part of the Dakota Territory. They wrote and ratified a state constitution that was approved by the U.S. Congress. On December 28, 1846, President James K. Polk signed a law making Iowa the 29th state. Iowa was admitted as a "free state"—one where slavery was not permitted. In 1857, the state capital was moved from Iowa City to Des Moines. By the 1860 census, nearly 675,000 people lived in Iowa.

The national disagreement over slavery would lead to the start of the American Civil War in April 1861. Iowa remained loyal to the Union, and was far from the fighting. However, the state contributed more than 75,000 soldiers for the Union Army, and over 13,000 died in the four-year conflict. Iowa farmers also provided much food for the army, as well as for civilians throughout the nation.

 Did You Know?

Iowa State University in Ames is the oldest "land grant college" in the United States. In 1862, a federal law called the Morrill Act allowed states to sell land owned by the federal government, and use the proceeds to support agricultural and mechanical research. Iowa was the first state to accept the provisions of the Morrill Act.

After the civil war ended, some freed slaves moved to Iowa, where they settled in communities near the Mississippi and Missouri Rivers, or worked on railroads or in the coal and lead mines near Dubuque. They joined immigrants from many other nations who were attracted to Iowa's farmland. State leaders actively encouraged immigrants to move to Iowa. By 1890, about one in every six Iowans had been born in another country. Most were from Germany, Ireland, and the Scandanavian countries of northern Europe.

The second half of the 19th centu-

This magazine illustration from 1861 shows the First Iowa Infantry Regiment charging into battle at Wilson's Creek, near Springfield, Missouri. General Nathanael Lyon, the first Union general killed in the Civil War, is depicted on horseback. Although no battles were fought in Iowa, troops from the state fought throughout the conflict.

Until major flooding occurred in 2008, Cedar Rapids was one of the few cities in America that had its municipal government facilities on an island. The Cedar Rapids city hall was located on Mays Island in the Cedar River. SInce the flooding, government offices have been moved to a former federal office building on the mainland.

ry also saw the development of industry in Iowa. Coal was needed to run trains and power steel mills, so mines were opened to exploit coal seams. Most of the coal mines were located in central and southern Iowa. Railroads were built across Iowa, allowing farm products to be shipped all over the United States. Facilities for slaughtering and processing meat, and for processing corn and other grains were opened throughout the state.

The outbreak of World War I in 1914 marked the start of a prosperous period for Iowa farmers, as food prices rose. Needing to produce extra food for the war effort, the U.S. government gave *subsidies* to farmers to keep the price of food low. This additional money encouraged farmers to purchase additional land and expand their farms. However, once the war ended in 1918 the government did away with these subsidies. Throughout the 1920s, many farmers struggled to pay debts they had incurred during the prosperous years. At the same time, the coal mining industry in Iowa began to decline. The

Henry Wallace, who would serve as the U.S. Secretary of Agriculture and Vice President, milks a cow on an Iowa farm.

state's economic problems grew worse with the start of the Great Depression in 1929, and lasted through the 1930s.

The New Deal policies of President Franklin D. Roosevelt provided some relief to Iowa farmers. Some of these had been proposed by Roosevelt's Secretary of Agriculture, Iowan Henry Wallace. However, the state's farmers did not truly recover from the depression until the 1940s, when farm prices were again fueled by a world war.

Iowa is still a major farm state, but

since the 1950s a greater number of industries have been established in the state.

In 1982, Terry Branstad was elected the governor of Iowa. He served four terms in that position, from 1983 until 1999. Branstad was re-elected governor in 2010 and 2014; if he completes his sixth term, he will be the longest-serving state governor in U.S. history.

Government

The Constitution of Iowa sets out the framework for the state's government. The current constitution was adopted in 1857, and has been amended 28 times since then, most recently in 2010.

The constitution provides for three branches of government in Iowa: the legislature, which makes the laws; the executive, which carries out the laws and oversees the day-to-day activities of the government; and the judicial, which rules on and interprets the laws.

The Iowa legislature includes two assemblies. The Iowa House of Representatives has 100 elected representatives, who are elected for two-year terms. The state Senate has 50 state senators, who are elected to four-year terms. There are no limits on the number of terms a person can serve in the legislature. As a result, some legislators are reelected many times. Both the Senate and House of Representatives must agree on a bill in order for it to become a state law. Sessions for both the House and Senate are held at the Iowa State Capitol building in Des Moines.

The governor is head of the executive branch of the state's government, and has the authority to appoint or remove the leaders of various branches of the state government. The governor is elected to a four-year term.

Several other elected state officers help to run the executive branch. They include the lieutenant governor and secretary of state, who help to run the executive branch; the state treasurer, who is the chief financial officer; and the attorney general, the state's chief legal official.

The judicial branch includes three levels of courts. Both civil and criminal cases are heard in district courts. Decisions in those cases can be appealed to the state's appellate courts. The highest court in the state is the Iowa Supreme Court, which consists of seven justices who serve eight-year terms.

In addition to the state government, county and local governments have the authority to levy taxes, pass legislation affecting their communities, and create and maintain local public infrastructure such as roads and bridges. Iowa has 99 counties and many smaller municipalities.

Iowa is represented in the federal government of the United States by two U.S. Senators and four members of the U.S. House of Representatives.

Did You Know?

The Broadway show *The Music Man* is set in the fictional Iowa community of River City. Show creator Meredith Wilson grew up in Mason City.

The Iowa state capitol building, completed in 1886, is unique in that it is the only U.S. capitol with five domes. The building houses the legislative chambers, as well as the office of the governor and other state officials.

Did You Know?

In 1959, an airplane crash near Clear Lake claimed the lives of three early rock-n-roll stars: Buddy Holly, Richie Valens, and J.P. "The Big Bopper" Richardson.

In presidential elections, the state casts six electoral votes. However, Iowa gets a lot of attention in presidential election years because it traditionally holds the first presidential *caucus* in the election cycle. These involve people gathering in homes or public places and choosing their candidates publicly. Because the winner of the Iowa caucus gains a lot of national media attention, presidential candidates often begin their campaigns by setting up headquarters in the state and spending a significant amount of time interacting with Iowa voters.

The Economy

Iowa is a farm state. The state has a relatively long, warm growing season and has deep, rich soil that is great for growing things. There are more than 88,600 farms in Iowa, and nearly 86 percent of the total land area, over 30 million acres (12.1 million hectares), is used for farming.

Corn has been the leading crop in Iowa for many years. Iowa farmers grow more corn (about 2.3 bushels in 2015) than any other U.S. state and many other countries. (Iowa produces about three times as much corn as Mexico, for example.) Other important agricultural products include soybeans, various grains, eggs, and milk.

Some of the corn and soybeans raised in Iowa is used to feed livestock. Iowa is the number-one state for pork production, and raises nearly one-third of the nation's hogs. Hog farming is a $7.5 billion-a-year business. Farmers also raise cattle and other livestock.

Manufacturing is another important sector of the state's economy, with many businesses related to farm work, such as food processing or the manufacture of farm tools or fertilizers. Major food processors include

ConAgra, Heinz, General Mills, and Quaker Oats. The meatpacking firm Tyson Foods has 11 facilities in Iowa. John Deere tractors and heavy machinery are built at factories in Ankeny, Davenport, and Dubuque. ALCOA has a plant in Riverdale that produces aluminum materials for the aerospace industry.

Iowa is also a leading state when it comes to renewable energy and biofuel production. The state has 39 plants that convert corn and other grains into ethanol. In northern and western Iowa, large "wind farms" have been built to take advantage of constant winds.

Iowa has interesting connections to the computer industry. During the 1930s, a physicist at Iowa State named John Vincent Atanasoff invented an early computer *prototype*. It was used to solve complicated math problems. During the mid-1980s, entrepreneurs Ted Waitt and Mike Hammond established Gateway Computer in Sioux City. Although the company eventually moved to

Dubuque has historically been a center for manufacturing in Iowa.

Iowa's Old Capitol Building, built in 1842 when Iowa City was the capital, today is a National Historic Landmark that is part of the University of Iowa's campus.

are often referred to generically as "Winnebagos."

The People

Iowa is one of the least racially diverse states in the nation. According to the U.S. Census Bureau, more than 92 percent of Iowa's 3.1 million residents are white. (Of these people, about 5 percent identify as Hispanic or Latino.) Only 3.3 percent are black or African American, while 2 percent are Asian.

In the nineteenth century the state went out of its way to encourage immigrants to settle. Today, however, relatively few recent immigrants move to Iowa. Only about 4.5 percent of the state's population under age 5 was born in another country, and just 7 percent speak a language other than English at home.

About 91 percent of Iowans graduate from high school, which is higher than the national average of 86 percent. However, they are slightly less likely to have earned a college degree (25.7 percent vs. the national average of 28.8 percent). To experts, this indi-

California's Silicon Valley, it retained a link to its heartland roots by shipping products in boxes with a distinctive black-and-white pattern similar to a Holstein cow.

Winnebago Industries was founded in Forest City in 1958. The company is perhaps the best known manufacturer of recreational vehicles, and even RVs made by other companies

The set for the 1989 movie Field of Dreams, located in Dyersville, is a popular tourist attraction.

cates that many young educated Iowans are leaving the state in search of better jobs.

The median household income is about $52,000, near the national average. The poverty rate in Iowa, at 12.4 percent, is a little lower than the nation as a whole (15.4 percent).

About 75 percent of Iowa residents describe themselves as Christian, with 52 percent following Protestant denominations (such as the Methodist and Lutheran churches) and 23 percent observing Roman Catholic doc-trines. About 13 percent of Iowans describe themselves as non-religious.

Major Cities

More than 207,000 people live in *Des Moines*, the capital city of Iowa. In addition to state government offices, Des Moines is home to many insurance companies and banks. The international headquarters of Principal Financial Group, a global investment firm, are located in the city's tallest building, a 45-story skyscraper.

The city has undergone many

Some Famous Iowans

There has been one U.S. President from Iowa. Herbert Hoover (1874–1964) was born in West Branch and lived in the state until he was about 11. Hoover held several important government positions before serving as president from 1929 to 1933. Hoover's successor, Franklin D. Roosevelt, chose another Iowan, Henry A. Wallace (1888–1965) to serve in his administration as Secretary of Agriculture, and later as vice president from 1941 to 1945. In the 1948 presidential election, Wallace was the candidate of the Progressive Party.

Herbert Hoover

American women have the right to vote thanks in part to Carrie Chapman Catt (1859–1947), who grew up on a farm in Iowa and attended Iowa State University. Catt served as president of the National American Woman Suffrage Association, which promoted passage of the Nineteenth Amendment in 1919. That year she founded the League of Women Voters, which continues to inform voters about the candidates running in national and state elections.

The famed Western actor John Wayne (1907–1979) was born Marion Morrison in Winterset, although his family moved to Los Angeles when he was nine. Wayne became an American icon through such films as *Rio Bravo* (1959), *The Man Who Shot Liberty Valance* (1962), and *True Grit* (1969).

Baseball Hall of Fame pitcher Bob Feller (1918–2010) was known as "The Heater from Van Meter" and "Rapid Robert" due to his overpowering fastball. Feller signed a contract with the Cleveland Indians while still a student at Van Meter High School in central Iowa. He would win 266 games in the major leagues, be selected to eight All-Star teams, and helped the Indians win the 1948 World Series.

Astronaut Peggy Whitson (b. 1960) grew up on a farm near Beaconsfield and attended Iowa Wesleyan College before being accepted into the space program. She has spent more time in space than any other female astronaut.

Peggy Whitson

changes over the past decade. In 2005, the new Science Center of Iowa and the Iowa Events Center were both opened. In 2006, the Des Moines Public Library moved into a new building. Des Moines also has a sky-walk system of glass-and-steel tunnels across the downtown roadways, which connects many buildings. The extensive system is 4 miles (6.4 km) long, and enables people to move from building to building without going outside.

In 2013, a 1.2 mile (0.8 km) recreational trail called the Principal Riverwalk was completed along the banks of the Des Moines River. Two pedestrian bridges connect the east and west sides of the downtown area, and there are botanical gardens, an ice-skating rink, fountains, and sculptures.

Cedar Rapids (population 128,000) is located in eastern Iowa. It is home to many museums and cultural centers, including the Cedar Rapids Museum of Art, the National Czech & Slovak Museum and Library, the Paramount Theatre, Cedar Rapids Theatre, and the Iowa Cultural

Teenagers exercise and show swine during a 4-H competition at the Iowa State Fair.

Corridor Alliance. The city is also home to minor-league baseball, hockey, and football teams.

Davenport (population 102,157) is located near the Iowa-Illinois border. It is part of the Quad Cities metropolitan area, which also includes the Iowa city of ***Bettendorf*** (population 34,000) as well as Rock Island, Moline, and East Moline in Illinois. Although Davenport is subject to regular flooding due to its position on the Mississippi River, it is also considered one of the nicest small cities to live in in the United States.

About 84,000 people live in *Sioux City*, which is located in northwestern Iowa at the navigational head of the Missouri River. The Sergeant Floyd Monument is a 100-foot (30 m) tall obelisk that marks the burial site of Charles Floyd, the only man to die on the Lewis and Clark Expedition.

Iowa City (population 72,000) was the capital when Iowa became a state in 1846. Today it is a college town, home to the University of Iowa. That university, the state's largest, enrolls more than 30,000 students. The Iowa Writer's Workshop is a world-famous creative-writing program hosted by the university. In athletics, Iowa is a member of the Big Ten conference. It is best known for its wrestling program, which has won 23 national titles since 1975.

Some other large communities in Iowa include *Council Bluffs* (population 62,000), which in the 19th century was the starting point for the Mormon Trail; *Ames* (population 62,000), home to Iowa State University; and *Dubuque* (population 59,000), near the border with Wisconsin and Illinois.

Further Reading

Blashfield, Jean F. *Iowa*. New York: Children's Press, 2014.

Marciniak, Kristin. *What's Great About Iowa?* Minneapolis: Lerner, 2015.

Ryan, Patrick. *Iowa: The Hawkeye State*. Minneapolis: Bellwether Media, 2013.

Internet Resources

http://www.iowahistory.org

The State Historical Society of Iowa preserves, manages, and provides access to the state's historical resources.

http://www.iowa.gov

This is the official website for the State of Iowa, and provides information about state and local government services.

http://www.traveliowa.com

The official tourism website of Iowa provides information about places to visit and things to do in the state.

http://www.americaslibrary.gov/es/ia/es_ia_subj.html

A page of interesting information about Iowa, provided by the Library of Congress.

 Text-Dependent Questions

1. What large, marshy area lies to the south of Iowa's highest point?
2. Why is Iowa politically important in national presidential elections every four years?
3. What are some of the major food processing companies in Iowa?

 Research Project

The Homestead Act of 1862 attracted throngs of immigrants to frontier areas of the country, including Iowa. Using the Internet or your school library, research the Homestead Act. Find out what the law required settlers to do in order to make a land claim. See if you can find first-hand accounts of 19th-century homesteaders.

Missouri at a Glance

Area: 69,707 sq mi (180,540 sq km). 21st largest state[1]
Land: 68,742 sq mi (178,040 sq km)
Water: 966 sq mi (2,501 sq km)
Highest elevation: Taum Sauk Mountain, 1,772 feet (540 m
Lowest elevation: St. Francis River at southern Arkansas border, 230 feet (70 m)

Statehood: Aug. 10, 1821 (24th state)
Capital: Jefferson City

Population: 6,063,589 (18th largest state)[2]

State nickname: the Show Me State
State bird: Eastern bluebird
State flower: *Crataegus punctata*

[1] *U.S. Geological Survey*
[2] *U.S. Census Bureau, 2014 estimate*

Missouri

D ue to its location in the center of the United States, and the similarity of its population demographics to national averages, for many years Missouri has been considered a *bellwether state* that could predict future economic and political trends in the United States.

Geography

Among the 48 contiguous states, Missouri is located close to the center. The state covers an area of 69,709 square miles (180,533 sq km). It is the 21st largest state by area. The Mississippi River forms Missouri's eastern border, separating it from Illinois, Kentucky, and Tennessee. Arkansas is located to the south, with Oklahoma, Kansas, and Nebraska to the west.

The northern region of Missouri, covering about one-third of the state, is made up of rolling plains, with many rivers and streams. Many of these waterways flow flow through steep valleys created by millennia of erosion. Water flows into the Mississippi River, which is skirted throughout by high bluffs, some of which are 400 to 600 feet (120 to 180 m) high. In general, the terrain is higher and rockier in northwestern Missouri than it is in the northeast.

The Ozark Plateau, stretching north from Arkansas, covers most of the remaining land in the state. This area includes the two highest points in the state: Taum Sauk Mountain at 1,772 feet (540 m), and Lead Hill at 1,744 feet (532 m). Most of the Ozark region is characterized by valleys, low hills with rounded summits, and open spaces allowing an unobstructed view of the sky.

Bagnell Dam was built on the Osage River in this region during the early 1930s. It created a large reservoir known as the Lake of the Ozarks, which covers 55,000 acres (22,000 ha). A hydroelectric facility at Bagnell Dam generates electricity for use in the region. Another large manmade lake in the Ozarks is Table Rock Lake, created by a dam on the White River that was built in the mid-1950s. This lake is popular among tourists who visit the nearby resort town of Branson.

The small projection of land in southeastern Missouri is part of the Mississippi Alluvial Plain. This region, covering about 3,000 square miles (7,800 sq km) features lowlands that are swampy in some areas. In this region, the Mississippi must be kept away from communities by levees to prevent flooding.

Despite these protective measures, Missouri is prone to devastating floods. In the spring and summer of

 Words to Understand in This Chapter

bellwether state—a state that, due to its location and population, can be used to predict or indicate economic or political trends.

latitude—the angular distance of a place north or south of the earth's equator, usually expressed in degrees and minutes.

Fall foliage covers the low hills of the Ozark Plateau.

The Missouri River, the longest river in the United States, crosses the state, flowing 430 miles (690 km) from Kansas City in the west to Jefferson City (pictured here) in the center of the state, and emptying into the Mississippi River just above St. Louis in the east. The state capitol building can be seen to the left in this photo.

Many of Missouri's rivers flow past high bluffs that were created by erosion over millions of years. The Klondike Park overlook is on the Missouri River near St. Charles.

1993, the Missouri and Mississippi rivers both experienced severe flooding, inundating farms and crops over a huge area of the Midwest. In June 2008, the Mississippi flooded again, with an even higher crest than in 1993. In the spring of 2011, heavy rains and unusually high levels of melting snow led to record floods on the Missouri River that affected communities along its course, including Kansas City, Jefferson City, and many smaller towns in the state.

The average January high temperature in Jefferson City, in central Missouri, is around 40°F (4°C), while temperatures in July and August average around 88°F (31°C). Missouri receives average rainfall of about 43 inches (110 cm), and about 12 inches (31 cm) of snow a year.

History

The land that today is Missouri was visited by the French explorers Marquette and Joliet in the 1670s, and claimed for France by La Salle in 1682. However, a permanent French settlement in Missouri was not established until around 1700, when a

French priest founded a mission near the point where the River Des Peres flows into the Mississippi.

French fur trappers and traders stopped at the small settlement for supplies, before heading into the wilderness. They encountered several Native American tribes in Missouri. The largest tribe was the Osage, who controlled most of the region between the Missouri and Red rivers. Many of their villages were located near the Osage River in southwestern Missouri. The Osage were friendly with the French. Tribes of the Illinois Confederacy, including the Kaskaskia and Peoria, also lived in northern Missouri. The Missouri Indians lived in villages along the Missouri River. However, this tribe was devastated by diseases inadvertently introduced by Europeans, such as smallpox.

For most of the period when the French controlled this region, there were few settlements in Missouri. The largest was the town of Ste. Genevieve, which was founded in 1735 but still only consisted of a few dozen houses by the early 1750s.

Inevitably, France came into conflict with Great Britain as Britain's American colonies sought to expand. In 1754, a dispute over control of the Ohio River valley touched off a major war. Battles took place not just in North America but around the globe. In Europe, the conflict was known as the Seven Years' War. American colonists would call it the French and Indian War.

By 1763, France was defeated. In the treaty ending the Seven Years' War, France ceded to Great Britain nearly all of its territory east of the Mississippi River. Spain took possession of France's territory west of the Mississippi, including Missouri.

St. Louis was established on high bluffs overlooking the Mississippi River in 1764. It, as well as other settlements in Missouri, expanded as French colonists left lands east of the Mississippi to escape British rule.

After the American Revolution, in which the 13 British colonies became independent, France regained its North American territory from Spain. But France did not keep this land, known as Louisiana, for long. In 1803, the French ruler Napoleon Bonaparte decided to sell Louisiana to the United States.

President Thomas Jefferson was eager to find out more about the vast Louisiana Territory. He sent an expedition commanded by Meriwether Lewis and William Clark to explore the new land. The expedition set out from St. Louis in 1804, and followed the Missouri River west to the Rocky Mountains. They eventually reached the Pacific Ocean, and returned to St. Louis in 1806.

The southernmost portion of the Louisiana Territory, including the port of New Orleans, was admitted to the Union as the state of Louisiana in 1812. To avoid confusion, the rest of the land was renamed the Missouri Territory. St. Louis became the capital of the Missouri Territory, which included not just Missouri but also the present-day states of Iowa, Kansas, Montana, Nebraska, North and South Dakota, Wyoming, and parts of Colorado and Minnesota.

Slavery had been established in Missouri long before the United States gained control of the territory. The first African-American slaves had been brought to Missouri by the Spanish to work in mines and on farms. However, Missouri would become an important battleground in the debate about slavery in the United States.

When Missouri asked to be considered for statehood in 1818, some northern leaders wanted slavery to be illegal there. At the time there was an equal number of slave and non-slave states, and people did not want to upset the political balance. The controversy was settled when Maine was broken away from Massachusetts and admitted as a free state at the same time as Missouri. It was then proposed that no more slave states would be created from territories north of Missouri's southern border (*latitude* line 36°30'). Congress passed this proposal, which came to be known as the Missouri Compromise. Along with the practice of admitting states in pairs—one slave, one free—in order to maintain the balance of power in the U.S. Senate, it would be a guiding principle of national politics for more than 30 years. However, the Missouri Compromise ultimately failed to prevent the debate over slavery from dividing the country.

In 1860 and early 1861, as southern states attempted to secede from the Union and form a new country, Missouri was one of four slave states that maintained allegiance to the United States during the Civil War.

Loyalties were divided in these so-called Border States. In 1862, Missouri had two governments that each claimed to be legitimate, one supporting the Union and the other supporting the rebellious Confederate States of America. About 110,000 Missouri men fought in the Union Army, while at least 30,000 others fought for the Confederacy. The Confederates made several attempts to gain control of the state, but were turned by Union forces in 1861 and again in 1864.

From 1862 to 1864, Missouri was the scene of a brutal guerrilla war between pro-Union supporters, known as Jayhawkers, and pro-Confederate supporters called Bushwackers. Often, neighbor fought against neighbor, especially along the Missouri-Kansas border.

Because Missouri had remained

During the late 1860s and 1870s, Missouri and the neighboring states were terrorized by the James Gang, which robbed banks, trains, and stagecoaches. Most of the gang's members, including Jessie James and brothers Cole, Jim, John, and Bob Younger, were from Missouri. This nineteenth-century postcard depicts the gang's 1868 robbery of a bank in Russellville, Kansas.

part of the Union during the Civil War, the Emancipation Proclamation of 1863 did not free slaves in the state. But near the end of the war the Missouri legislature passed legislation outlawing slavery.

Unfortunately, relations between blacks and whites in Missouri would continue to be uneasy over the next 150 years. As in other former slave states, blacks were often prevented from voting due to Jim Crow laws and literacy tests. The state was the site of several race riots, most notably one that occurred in East St. Louis in 1917. Segregation of schools and public facilities was enforced in Missouri until the Supreme Court ruled such practices illegal.

In August 2014, an 18-year-old black man named Michael Brown was shot and killed by a police officer in Ferguson, a suburb of St. Louis. The incident sparked protests in Ferguson, that soon spread to other cities. The National Guard was called in to prevent further violence, and federal authorities investigated the matter. In March 2015, the U.S. Justice Department announced it had determined that the Ferguson Police Department had acted inappropriately in the way it dealt with African Americans in Ferguson.

Government

The current constitution of Missouri was adopted in 1945, and creates a framework for the state government that has three branches: the legislature, which makes the laws; the executive, which carries out the laws and oversees the day-to-day activities of the government; and the judicial, which rules on and interprets the laws.

Like most states, Missouri's General Assembly includes two houses. The Missouri House of Representatives has 163 elected members, while the State Senate consists of 34 members. All legislators are subject to term limits. Members of the house can serve four two-year terms, while senators can serve two four-year terms. Both the Senate and House of Representatives must agree on a bill in order for it to become a state law. Legislative sessions are held during certain periods at the Missouri State Capitol building in Jefferson City.

The state governor is head of the executive branch of the state's government, and has the authority to appoint or remove the leaders of various branches of the state government. The governor is elected to a four-year term, and can serve two terms. A lieutenant governor, also elected to a four-year term, helps to run the executive branch and also casts a vote when there is a tie in the State Senate. If the governor resigns or dies while in office, the lieutenant governor assumes that position.

Several other executive officers are elected by voters in Missouri, including the secretary of state, state treasurer, attorney general, and state auditor.

The judicial branch includes three levels of courts. Both civil and criminal cases are heard in the state's 45 circuit courts, or in lower courts associated with each circuit. Decisions in those cases can be appealed to the Missouri Court of Appeals. The highest court in the state is the Supreme

Protesters march against racism after the shooting death of Michael Brown in Ferguson.

Court of Missouri, which consists of seven justices who serve twelve-year terms. Judges in Missouri must retire when they reach age 70.

In addition to the state government, county and local governments have the authority to levy taxes, pass legislation affecting their communities, and create and maintain local public infrastructure such as roads and bridges. Missouri has 114 counties and many smaller municipalities. The city of St. Louis is an independent city, and is not within the limits of a county.

Missouri is represented in the federal government of the United States by two U.S. Senators and eight members of the U.S. House of Representatives. In presidential elections, the state casts 10 electoral votes.

The Economy

In terms of agricultural production, Missouri is among the leading states. It has more than 100,000 farms, which produce beef, soybeans, pork, dairy products, hay, corn, poultry, sorghum, cotton, rice, and eggs.

The state has a vibrant mining and stone quarrying industry. Lead mines in east-central Missouri are the most productive in the nation. Missouri also produces more limestone, which is used to make cement, than any other state.

Many large businesses are headquartered in Missouri, producing aerospace equipment and chemicals, processing food, and brewing beer. Anheiser-Busch, founded in 1852 in St. Louis, operates 12 breweries throughout the United States. Monsanto, which conducts genetic research, is also based in St. Louis.

Tourism is another important sector of Missouri's economy. Many people come to the state to see the Gateway Arch and other interesting landmarks and sites.

The People

By 2015, the population of Missouri had grown to more than 6 million. This made it the 18th-largest state in the United States.

According to the U.S. Census Bureau, about 84 percent of Missouri residents are white. Blacks or African Americans make up 11.7 percent of the population. There are relatively small numbers of people of other races, such as Asians (1.8 percent) and Native Americans (0.5 percent).

Although Missouri was once a jumping-off point for pioneers moving West, today the state attracts relatively few immigrants. Residents who identify themselves as Hispanic or Latino (and can therefore be either racially white or black) compose less than 4 percent of the population, well below the national average of 17 percent. Only about 3.9 percent of the

Busch Stadium, home of the Saint Louis Cardinals, is filled to capacity during a game against their cross-state rivals the Kansas City Royals. The Royals, who play in the American League, reached the World Series in 2014, only to lose in seven games. The National League's Cardinals have won 11 World Series titles, most recently in 2011.

state's population under age 5 was born in another country, and just 6 percent speak a language other than English at home.

People in Missouri graduate from high school at a slightly higher rate than the national average (87.6 percent vs. 86 percent). However, they are slightly less likely to earn a college degree (26.2 percent vs. the national average of 28.8 percent). The median household income is about $47,400, slightly below the national average of $53,000. About 15 percent of Missouri residents have incomes below the federal poverty level, which is essentially the same as the national average.

Like Arkansas and other Southern states, Missouri is considered part of the Bible Belt. About 77 percent of Arkansas residents describe themselves as Christian, with the Baptist and Methodist churches being the largest denominations. About 19 percent are Roman Catholic. Roughly 15 percent of Missouri residents describe themselves as non-religious.

In the 19th century members of the Church of Jesus Christ of Latter-day Saints, also known as the Mormon Church or LDS Church, settled in Missouri before moving west to Utah. The LDS Church, as well as some related denominations that broke away from the main church, still have sizeable communities in the city of Independence.

Major Cities

Missouri's largest city is **Kansas City**, which is located on the Missouri River at the border with Kansas. It covers 316 square miles (820 sq km). Kansas City is known for its distinctive style of jazz music, which originated in the 1930s, as well as for its steakhouses and barbecue restaurants.

Today Kansas City has a population of about 467,000. The Kansas City metropolitan area, which includes suburbs in both Kansas and Missouri, has a population of about 2.34 million.

The city of **St. Louis** was founded in 1764, and during the nineteenth century it was a major port on the Mississippi River. The Gateway Arch,

The U.S. government is the largest employer in Kansas City, as nearly 150 different federal agencies have offices there. The Internal Revenue Services (IRS), which collects taxes for the federal government, has an enormous processing center in Kansas City. Other federal agencies are housed at the Bannister complex in the southern part of the city.

a 630-foot (192-m) tall steel monument, commemorates the city's important role in the westward expansion of the United States.

St. Louis is home to many businesses and manufacturing firms. It is also home to three professional sports teams. The Cardinals are one of Major League Baseball's most successful franchises, having won 11 World Series championships. The city also hosts the NFL's Rams and the NHL's Blues. Today, the city is home to about 320,000 people; the metropolitan area, which includes suburbs in both Missouri and Illinois, has a population of about 2.95 million.

Springfield, located in southwestern Missouri, is the state's third-largest city with a population of about 164,000. The city was the site of several battles during the Civil War. Today, the city is home to the Positronic manufacturing facility, as well as the national headquarters of retailers Bass Pro Shops and O'Reilly Auto Parts. The famed Route 66, which connected Chicago to Los Angeles, once ran through Springfield.

 Did You Know?

Kansas City offers a variety of museums and other attractions, including the Kansas City Zoo; the National World War I Museum at Liberty Memorial; the Negro Leagues Baseball Museum; and the Kemper Museum of Contemporary Art.

Independence, a suburb of Kansas City, is known as "Queen City of the Trails," because during the 19th century it was the final point of departure for many immigrants headed West. It was also the birthplace of U.S. President Harry S. Truman, and the Truman Presidential Library and Museum is located in the city. Today, the city has a population of about 118,000.

Harry S. Truman

Columbia (population 115,000) is the county seat for Boone County and home to several colleges, including the University of Missouri, Stephens College, and Columbia College. The

Some Famous Missourians

One of America's greatest authors was Samuel Clemens (1835–1910), better known by the pen name Mark Twain. His childhood in Hannibal provided the setting for his famous novels *The Adventures of Tom Sawyer* (1876) and *The Adventures of Huckleberry Finn* (1885).

Mark Twain

The African-American scientist George Washington Carver (1864?–1943) was into slavery in Diamond Grove. He became the first black student at Iowa State University, and later became head of the agricultural department at Tuskegee Institute in Alabama. During his 47 years there, Carver was involved in researching and promoting crop alternatives to cotton, such as peanuts, soybeans, and sweet potatoes.

Molly Brown

Hannibal native Margaret "Molly" Tobin Brown (1867–1932) was a passenger on the doomed ocean liner Titanic in April 1912. She survived the sinking on a lifeboat, and encouraged the crew to look for survivors in the water. Her exploits led her to be nick-named "the Unsinkable Molly Brown."

Legendary rock guitarist Chuck Berry (b. 1926) grew up in St. Louis. Known for hits like "Johnny B. Goode" and "Maybellene," Berry was one of the first musicians inducted into the Rock and Roll Hall of Fame, in 1986.

Ginger Rodgers (1911–1995) was an actress, dancer and singer who appeared in more than 70 films. She is best known for a series of musical films made with Fred Astaire during the 1930s, and won the Oscar for Best Actress in 1940 for her role in *Kitty Foyle*.

Politician John Ashcroft (b. 1942) served as governor of Missouri from 1985 to 1993, represented the state in the U.S. Senate from 1995 to 2001), and served as U.S. Attorney General in the George W. Bush administration from 2001 to 2005. After leaving public office, he started a consulting firm.

city is also home to healthcare and insurance firms, as well as the State Historical Society of Missouri. In recent years the city's population has grown considerably.

During the 19th century, *St. Joseph* was an important stopping point for pioneers who were headed west on the Oregon Trail. It also was the eastern terminal for the Pony Express, a short-lived mail service to California in 1860 and 1861. The former stables are now the Pony Express Museum. Today, this city on the Missouri River has a population of around 77,000.

The state capital, *Jefferson City*, is a small city with a population of about 43,000. It is located in central Missouri, on the southern side of the Missouri River. In addition to numerous government buildings, Jefferson City is home to Lincoln University, which was founded in 1866 to educate freed African-American slaves. Not far from the city is Missouri's grape-growing and wine-making region, known as the Missouri Rhineland because the vineyards were originally planted by German settlers.

In recent years *Branson* has become a nationally famous tourist destination, thanks to its many entertainment theaters featuring country music performers, as well as Silver Dollar City, a nearby theme park. The city has a population of about 10,500.

Further Reading

Blashfield, Jean F. *Missouri*. New York: Children's Press, 2014.

Marsh, Carole. *I'm Reading About Missouri*. Peachtree, Ga.: Gallopade International, 2014.

Oachs, Emily Rose. *Missouri: The Show-Me State*. Minneapolis: Bellwether Media, 2013.

Internet Resources

http://www.americaslibrary.gov/es/mo/es_mo_subj.html

A page of interesting information about Missouri, provided by the Library of Congress.

http://www.mo.gov

The official government website for the Show Me State provides information about state and local government services.

http://www.visitmo.com

The official tourism website of Missouri provides information about places to visit and things to do in the state.

http://shs.umsystem.edu/index.shtml

The State Historical Society of Missouri provides materials related to the state's history, geneaological information, and has several digital collections available at its website.

 # Text-Dependent Questions

1. Where is Bagnell Dam? What large reservoir did it create?
2. In what year was the city of St. Louis founded? In what Missouri county is it located?
3. What are some of Missouri's most important agricultural products?

 # Research Project

Using your school library or the internet, find out more about the Missouri Compromise of 1820. Why was it politically important to maintain an equal balance between free and slave states? When and why was the Missouri Compromise superseded, and what was the result? Write a short essay on the Missouri Compromise and present your findings to your class.

Index

Numbers in **bold italics** refer to captions.

Series Glossary of Key Terms

bicameral—having two legislative chambers (for example, a senate and a house of representatives).

cede—to yield or give up land, usually through a treaty or other formal agreement.

census—an official population count.

constitution—a written document that embodies the rules of a government.

delegation—a group of persons chosen to represent others.

elevation—height above sea level.

legislature—a lawmaking body.

precipitation—rain and snow.

term limit—a legal restriction on how many consecutive terms an office holder may serve.